# RECORD BREAKERS
# CARS

## DANIEL GILPIN

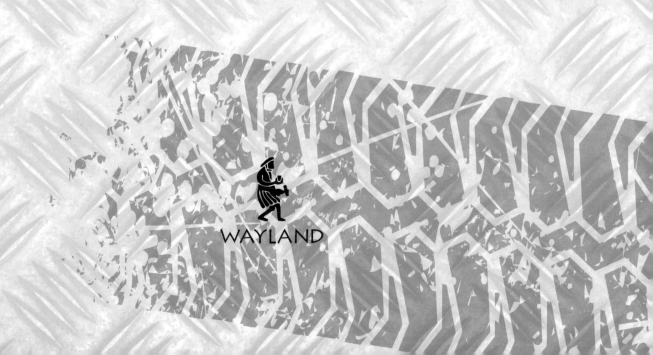

WAYLAND

First published in 2010 by Wayland

Copyright © Wayland 2010

Wayland
338 Euston Road
London NW1 3BH

Wayland Australia
Level 17/207 Kent Street
Sydney NSW 2000

Senior Editor: Debbie Foy
Designer: Rob Walster
Picture Researcher: Kate Lockley

British Library Cataloguing in Publication Data:
Gilpin, Daniel.
   Record breakers.
   Cars.
   1. Automobiles--Miscellanea--Juvenile
literature.
   2. World records--Juvenile literature.
   I. Title
   629.2'22-dc22

ISBN: 9780750262750

Printed in China

Wayland is a division of
Hachette Children's Books,
an Hachette UK company.

www.hachette.co.uk

## Picture credits:

Andia/Alamy: 6B
Geoff Caddick/Rex Features: 26-27
Car Culture/Corbis: 18-19
© Daimler AG: 10BL
Martyn Goddard/Corbis: 28-29
Hennessey Venom 1000 twin turbo Dodge Viper SRT
engine, © Hennessey Performance: 20BC
PATRICK HERZOG/AFP/Getty Images: 28B
Inspiration Steam Car Co: 24-25, 30
Carolyn Kaster/AP/Press Association Images: Cover, 6-7
Tony Lewis/Getty Images: 8-9
© Chris Littler,  HYPERLINK "http://www.chrislittler.net"
www.chrislittler.net: 26B
Morgan Motor Company: 22-23
Motoring Picture Library/Alamy: 5TR, 15
© Nuon Solar Team: 8B
Pagani Automobili SpA: 10-11
© 2008 SSC, Inc. All Rights Reserved: 2, 16-17
Sipa Press/Rex Features: 12C
David Taylor/Allsport/Getty Images: 13
© Toyota Europe: 14
Transtock/Alamy: 4-5, 20-21

## Abbreviations used:

m = metres
km = kilometres
ft = feet
in = inches
cm = centimetres
mph = miles per hour
km/h = kilometres per hour
hp = horsepower
kg = kilogrammes
lb = pounds

Tricky words are listed in 'But What
Does That Mean?' on page 31.

# WHAT'S INSIDE?

# BUGATTI VEYRON

The Bugatti Veyron speeds up faster than any other car on the road. In a race from 0–97 km (0–60 miles) per hour, it would leave the world's fastest road car behind!

## Can you believe it?

The Bugatti Veyron is a four-wheel drive, just like the Land Rover. This is unusual for sports cars because most are two-wheel drive.

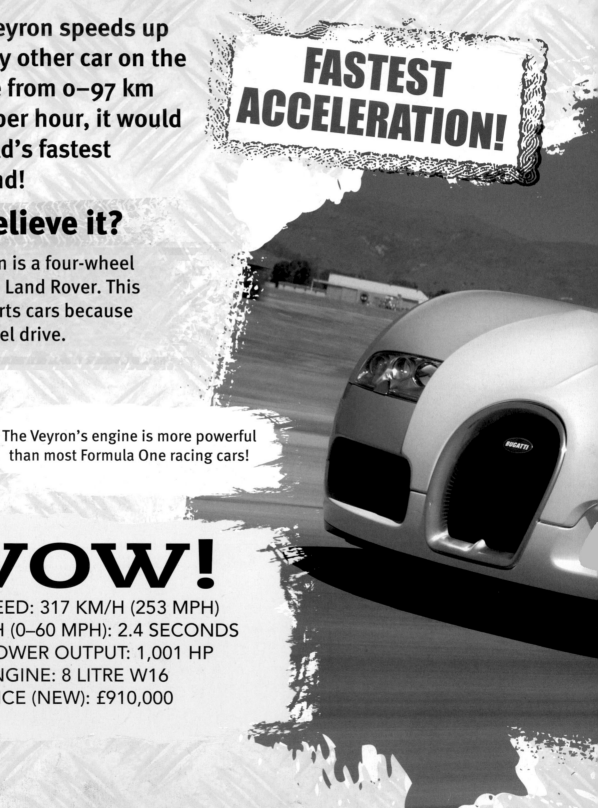

**FASTEST ACCELERATION!**

The Veyron's engine is more powerful than most Formula One racing cars!

# WOW!

TOP SPEED: 317 KM/H (253 MPH)
0–97 KM/H (0–60 MPH): 2.4 SECONDS
MAX POWER OUTPUT: 1,001 HP
ENGINE: 8 LITRE W16
PRICE (NEW): £910,000

The Bugatti Veyron's interior is designed for comfort and luxury.

# HUMMER H1 ALPHA WAGON

The H1 Alpha Wagon is the world's largest production car. It was adapted from the Humvee military vehicle, which was designed for off-road operations and is used by the US Army.

## Can you believe it?

The H1 Alpha Wagon does just 19 km (12 miles) per gallon. Hummer stopped making it in 2006, when new laws in the US made such low levels illegal.

There are also convertible and pick-up versions of the H1 Alpha Wagon.

The Alpha Wagon clears the ground by a huge 40 cm (16 in)!

# WOW!

LENGTH: 4.67 M (15 FT, 4 IN)
WIDTH: 2.18 M (7 FT, 2 IN)
WEIGHT: 3,684 KG (8,114 LB)
TOP SPEED: 145 KM/H (90 MPH)
ENGINE: 6.6 LITRE V8 TURBODIESEL

# NUNA 2

Nuna 2 is the world's fastest solar-powered car. Using nothing but the energy from sunlight, it can reach speeds of more than 160 km (100 miles) per hour!

## Can you believe it?

To reach 100 km (60 miles) per hour, Nuna 2 needs just 1,650 watts of electricity. This is the same amount of power that is used by a hairdryer!

The 'pilot' needs to be in a lying down position to drive Nuna 2.

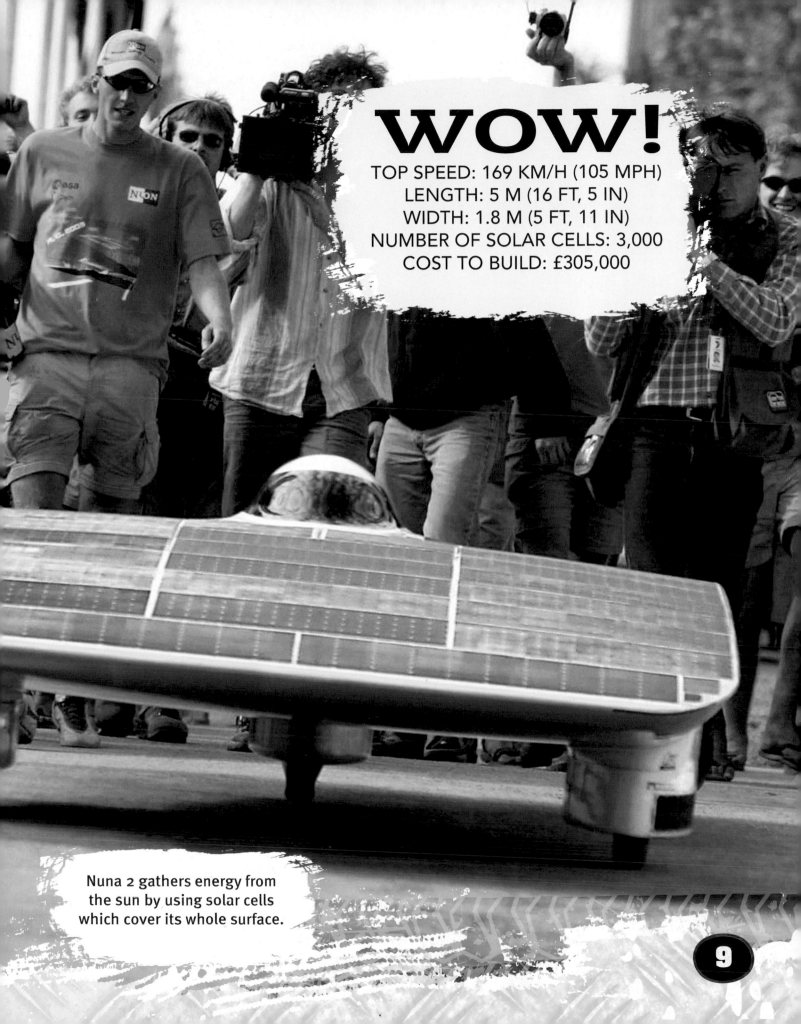

# WOW!

TOP SPEED: 169 KM/H (105 MPH)
LENGTH: 5 M (16 FT, 5 IN)
WIDTH: 1.8 M (5 FT, 11 IN)
NUMBER OF SOLAR CELLS: 3,000
COST TO BUILD: £305,000

Nuna 2 gathers energy from the sun by using solar cells which cover its whole surface.

# PAGANI ZUNDA TRICOLORE

**This amazing car costs more to buy new than any other car ever made!**

## Can you believe it?

Only one Pagani Zonda Tricolore was ever made! It was built in 2010 to celebrate the 50th anniversary of the Italian Red Arrows.

Before the Zonda Tricolore was built, the record was held for 12 years by the Mercedes Benz CLK/LM.

# WOW!

TOP SPEED: 349 KM/H (217 MPH)
0–97 KM/H (0–60 MPH): 3.4 SECONDS
MAX POWER OUTPUT: 678 HP
ENGINE: 7.3 LITRE V12
PRICE (NEW): £1,340,000

# On the other hand...

With only one ever made, the Zonda Tricolore is also the world's rarest supercar!

Built in India, the Tata Nano is the world's cheapest production car. When it first went on sale in 2009, it cost just 123,000 rupees (£1,615).

# THRUST SSC

Thrust SSC is the fastest car on Earth! On 13 October 1997, it became the first car to go faster than the speed of sound. And two days later, this amazing car set a new land speed record!

## Can you believe it?

Thrust SSC has the same engine power as 145 Formula One racing cars – or 1,000 Ford Escorts!

Thrust SSC during its record-breaking run. It was driven here by a Royal Air Force pilot.

## CONTENDERS

The Thrust SSC team are now developing another jet-powered car. It is called Bloodhound SSC and is designed to travel at more than 1,600 km (over 1,000 miles) per hour!

Thrust SSC's engines were developed for jet fighter planes.

# WOW!

TOP SPEED: 317 KM/H (763 MPH)
MAX POWER OUTPUT: 110,000 HP
LENGTH: 16.5 M (54 FT)
WEIGHT: 10,500 KG (23,153 LB)
ENGINES: TWO ROLLS ROYCE
SPEY 205 JET ENGINES

# TUYOTA CURULLA

The Toyota Corolla is the world's best-selling car. Since it was first made in 1966, 35 million of them have been sold!

## Can you believe it?

On average, there has been one new Toyota Corolla sold every 40 seconds, for the past 40 years!

# WOW!

NUMBER SOLD: 35 MILLION
COUNTRIES PRODUCING: 15
TOP SPEED: 211 KM/H (131 MPH)
0–97 KM/H (0–60 MPH): 7.8 SECONDS
NAME IN BRITAIN: TOYOTA AURIS

# BUGATTI 'ROYALE' TYPE 41

The Bugatti 'Royale' Type 41 was designed and built to transport royalty. Only six of these huge cars were ever made!

## Can you believe it?

This car cost much more second-hand than any new car ever did. In 1990, a used Bugatti 'Royale' sold for US$15 million (£8.6 m)!

**MOST EXPENSIVE EVER!**

# WOW!

NUMBER BUILT: 6
YEARS MADE: 1929–1933
LENGTH: 6.4 M (21 FT)
WEIGHT: 3,175 KG (7,001 LB)
PRICE NEW (IN 1930): £9,150

# ULTIMATE AERO TT

The Ultimate Aero is the world's fastest production car. The record-breaking TT (Twin Turbo) version came out in 2007, and can reach an incredible 412 km (256 miles) per hour!

## Can you believe it?

There are plans to build an electric version (or EV) of the Ultimate Aero. This will challenge the record for the world's fastest electric car. The EV is expected to reach speeds of 335 km (208 miles) per hour!

**FASTEST ROAD CAR!**

The speed record was set on the Shelby SuperCars test track in the United States.

The Ultimate Aero TT has amazing 'butterfly wing' doors!

# WOW!

TOP SPEED: 412 KM/H (256 MPH)
0–97 KM/H (0–60 MPH): 2.8 SECONDS
MAX POWER OUTPUT: 1,287 HP
ENGINE: 6.3 LITRE V8 TWIN TURBO
PRICE (NEW): £335,000

# VW L1

The VW L1 is the world's most fuel-efficient car. It has a small diesel engine combined with an electric motor. Its streamlined body keeps fuel use down.

## Can you believe it?

The VW L1 is more than just a concept car. It should be on our roads by 2013!

## On the other hand...

The world's least fuel-efficient road car is the Lamborghini Murcielago. In city traffic, it does an average of 12 km (8 miles) per gallon.

# WOW!

MILES PER GALLON: 189
TOP SPEED: 159 KM/H (99 MPH)
0–97 KM/H (0–60 MPH):
14.3 SECONDS
MAX POWER OUTPUT: 29 HP
ENGINE: 0.8 LITRE
TURBODIESEL HYBRID

The VW L1 is designed to carry two people, one behind the other.

The sleek VW L1 weighs just 380 kg (840 lb)!

# DODGE VIPER SRT-10

The Dodge Viper SRT-10 has the biggest engine of any production car. Its engine is so loud that you can hear a Dodge Viper coming a long time before you can see it!

## Can you believe it?

The Viper's engine was based on the Chrysler LA, which is an engine used in American trucks.

The 10-cylinder Viper engine has powerful twin turbos.

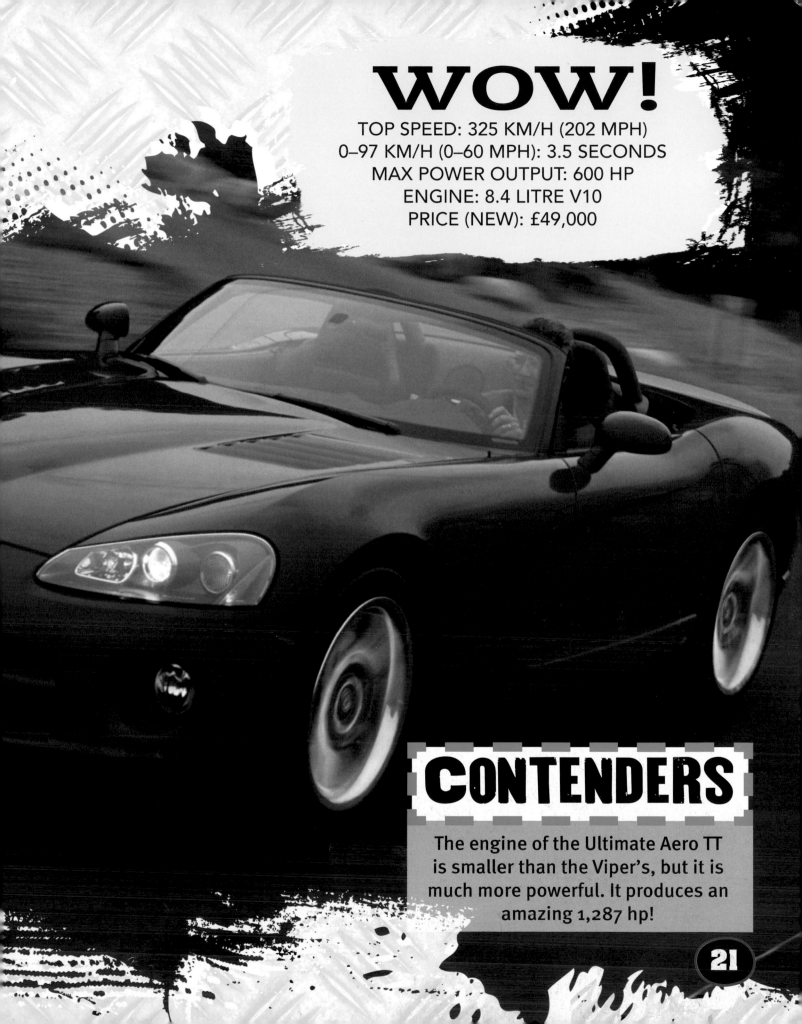

# WOW!

TOP SPEED: 325 KM/H (202 MPH)
0–97 KM/H (0–60 MPH): 3.5 SECONDS
MAX POWER OUTPUT: 600 HP
ENGINE: 8.4 LITRE V10
PRICE (NEW): £49,000

## CONTENDERS

The engine of the Ultimate Aero TT is smaller than the Viper's, but it is much more powerful. It produces an amazing 1,287 hp!

# MORGAN 4/4

The Morgan 4/4 was first built in 1936. New cars are still being made at the original factory site, in the heart of the English countryside.

## Can you believe it?

The 4/4 was the first four-wheeled car built by Morgan. Before 1936, the Morgan company only built three-wheelers!

**OLDEST STILL MADE!**

'4/4' stands for 4 wheels and 4 cylinders!

# WOW!

TOP SPEED: 185 KM/H (115 MPH)
0–97 KM/H (0–60 MPH):
8 SECONDS
ENGINE: 1.8 LITRE 4-CYLINDER
PRICE IN 1936: £194
PRICE TODAY: £27,000

With the top down, you can see the 4/4's fine leather interior.

## CONTENDERS

The design of the original VW Beetle was unchanged from 1938 until 2003. The last VW Beetles to be sold were built in Mexico.

# INSPIRATION

Inspiration is the world's fastest steam-powered car. On 27 August 2009, a new world record was set on a desert track in California.

## Can you believe it?

The British-made Inspiration broke the world record held since 1906 by the American Stanley Steamer. At that time, the Stanley Steamer was the fastest land vehicle on Earth. It was also the first land vehicle ever to travel at more than 200 km (124 miles) per hour.

The British Inspiration team, with their record-breaking car.

# WOW!

TOP SPEED: 243 KM/H (151 MPH)
MAX POWER OUTPUT: 360 HP
LENGTH: 7.66 M (25 FT, 2 IN)
WIDTH: 1.7 M (5 FT, 7 IN)
WEIGHT: 3,051 KG (6,720 LB)

Inspiration is put through its paces in the Californian desert.

# PEEL P50

The Peel P50 is the world's smallest production car. It was only built during 1963–64, and its tiny engine was first designed to power mopeds.

## Can you believe it?

The P50 has no reverse gear. To turn the car around, the driver gets out and lifts the car up using a handle on the back!

# WOW!

LENGTH: 1.34 M (4 FT, 5 IN)
WIDTH: 0.99 M (3 FT, 3 IN)
WEIGHT: 59 KG (130 LB)
TOP SPEED: 61 KM/H (38 MPH)
ENGINE: 0.05 LITRE, TWO-STROKE

The P50 was built on the Isle of Man – where there is no speed limit!

NOW MANY WILL IT TAKE?

The former world's smallest man sits in the world's smallest production car.

# CONTENDERS

Some one-off, home-made cars are even smaller than the P50. Perhaps the smallest is Wind-up, built by car fanatic Perry Watkins. It is less that half the size of the P50!

# LAMBORGHINI GALLARDO

The Lamborghini Gallardo is one of the world's fastest and most expensive cars. Two of them zoom around on the streets of Rome, Italy, as police cars!

## Can you believe it?

Each of Rome's police Gallardos are fitted with a small fridge! They are used to carry human organs needed for transplant operations.

Rome's police Gallardos are fully equipped with radios and speed detectors.

## CONTENDERS

Other countries also have super-fast police cars. In Germany, the fastest is a Brabus CLS V12, nicknamed The Rocket. In Austria, some police officers drive the Porsche 911.

# WOW!

TOP SPEED: 317 KM/H (197 MPH)
0–97 KM/H (0–60 MPH): 4.1 SECONDS
MAX POWER OUTPUT: 552 HP
ENGINE: 5.2 LITRE V10
PRICE (NEW): £140,300

# TEST YOURSELF!

Can you remember facts about the record-breaking cars in this book? Test yourself here by answering these questions!

1. Which car is bigger, a Peel P50 or a Hummer H1 Alpha Wagon?

2. Which Italian city has Lamborghini police cars?

3. What car made US$15 million (£8.6 m) when it was sold in 1990?

4. In which year did Thrust SSC set the world land speed record?

5. How many Corollas have been sold throughout the world?

6. When was the Pagani Zonda Tricolore built?

7. Which is quicker from 0–97 km/h (0–60 mph), the Ultimate Aero TT or the Bugatti Veyron?

8. In which country is the Morgan 4/4 made?

9. Was the Stanley Steamer an American or a British car?

10. Which country was the last one to make new VW Beetles?

**Answers**

1. A Hummer H1 Alpha Wagon
2. Rome
3. A Bugatti 'Royale' Type 41
4. 1997
5. 35 million
6. 2010
7. The Bugatti Veyron
8. England
9. An American car
10. Mexico

# BUT WHAT DOES THAT MEAN?

**acceleration**   How fast a car speeds up.

**concept car**   A one-off car, built to test out an idea, but usually not for sale.

**convertible**   A car with a fold-away roof.

**cylinders**   The parts of a car's engine where the fuel is lit, and turned into energy and carried to the wheels.

**fanatic**   A person who is devoted to an activity or hobby.

**hp**   The power of a car's engine is measured in horsepower. The higher the horsepower of an engine, the more powerful it is.

**hybrid**   A car that uses a combination of petrol (or diesel) and electric power.

**illegal**   This means against the law.

**interior**   The inside of a car.

**litre**   A measurement of volume. The size of a car's engine (the total volume of its cylinders) is measured in litres.

**max power output**   The maximum amount of power that a car's engine can make and carry to the wheels.

**off-road**   Cars that are built to travel off public roads and over rough ground.

**pick-up**   A truck with an open back.

**production car**   A car made in a factory and sold for use on the road.

**reverse gear**   The gear on a car that allows it to go backwards.

**solar car**   A car powered by electricity, made by solar cells on its bodywork.

**solar cell**   A tiny device used for turning the energy from sunlight into electricity.

**speed of sound**   The speed that sound travels through the air, which is 1,225 km (761 miles) per hour!

**streamlined**   A vehicle with a smooth shape, which allows air to flow freely over it and so travel faster!

**transplant**   To implant an organ into another person's body.

**used**   Another word for second-hand.

**v10**   An engine with 10 cylinders arranged in a V shape. A V12 engine has 12 cylinders arranged in a V shape.

**w16**   An engine with 16 cylinders arranged in a W shape.

# CHECK IT OUT & INDEX

## Check out these amazing places to go and websites to visit!

**National Motor Museum, Beaulieu, England**
One of Britain's top motor museums.

**Museum of British Road Transport, Coventry, England**
Visit this museum to see Thrust SSC!

**ZAZ Automotive Museum, Nagoya, Japan**
One of the world's few 'supercar' museums.

**Black Rock Desert, Nevada, USA**
Where the Thrust CC land speed record attempt took place in 1997.

**http://www.shelbysupercars.com**
Internet home of Shelby SuperCars, makers of the Ultimate Aero TT.

**http://www.bugatti.com**
The official Bugatti website. Includes lots of great pictures and information about the Veyron and the 'Royale'.

**http://www.thrustssc.com**
Official website of the Thrust SSC team.

## Index

# RECORD BREAKERS

## Contents of titles in the series:

WAYLAND